D0572919

Alamo plaza, circa 1885

Entry to the Alamo chapel after 1850

THE ALAMO

LEONARD EVERETT FISHER

Holiday House / New York

The northwest corner of the Alamo, with a view
of the Long Barrack in the foreground

A nearly full moon lit the Alamo and the flat Texas ground upon which the old mission sat. A few dark clouds drifted overhead. Moonlight kept the blackness out of the cold March night. So, too, did the campfires that flared among the Mexican troops. The soldiers shivered in the brisk air, waiting for the order to storm the Alamo and its one hundred eighty-eight Texan defenders. Texas, a province of Mexico, would soon declare its independence. Now it would fight for that freedom.

"To the people of Texas & all Americans in the world," said the letter dated February 24, 1836. "Fellow citizens and compatriots," the letter went on, "I am besieged, by a thousand or more of the Mexicans under Santa Anna—I have sustained a continual bombardment & cannonade for 24 hours & have not lost a man—The enemy has demanded a surrender at discretion, otherwise the garrison are to be put to the torch, if the fort is taken—I have answered the demand with a cannon shot, & our flag still waves proudly from the walls—I shall never surrender or retreat. Then, I call on you in the name of liberty, of patriotism & everything dear to the American character, to come to our aid with all dispatch—the enemy is receiving reinforcements daily & will no doubt increase to three or four thousand in four or five days. If this call is neglected, I am determined to sustain myself as long as possible & die like a soldier who never forgets what is due to his own honor & that of his country—." The letter was signed in "Victory or death" by Lieutenant Colonel William Barret Travis, Commander.

Now it was Sunday, March 6. The four thousand Mexican troops that Colonel Travis (1809–1836) had expected were before him. General Antonio López de Santa Anna Pérez de Lebron (1794–1876), president of Mexico and the commander of his own army, had already issued his instructions the day before:

Facade of the Alamo church after 1850

General Order of March 5th, 1836, 2:00 P.M. To the Generals, Chiefs of Sections and Corps Commanders:

Being necessary to act decisively upon the enemy defending The Alamo, the Most Excellent General-in-Chief has ordered that tomorrow at four o'clock the attacking columns, placed at short distance from the first trenches, undertake the assault to begin with a signal given by the General by means of the sounding of a bugle from the North Battery. . . .

General Santa Anna waited an extra hour. At five in the morning on March 6, the sharp, quick notes of a bugle split the cold night air. Soon, other bugles took up the blood-curdling rhythms. It was the sound of the Deguello, the call to show no mercy, to take no prisoners, to kill every defender of the Alamo. Immediately, fifteen hundred Mexican soldiers began moving against the Alamo. The mix of bugles, pounding feet, cannon thuds and crackling rifle fire, metal against stone and wood, shouts, and explosions tore up the stillness of dawn. An hour and a half later, at 6:30 A.M., all one hundred eighty-eight Texans inside the Alamo were dead.

Six hundred soldiers of Santa Anna's attacking force lay dead, as well. Spared were the wives, children, and servants of some of the Alamo defenders.

Since that Sunday in March 1836, the Alamo battleground in San Antonio, Texas, has become an American shrine—a place made sacred by the ordinary people who fought and died on its ground for Texas independence. Their battle set an example of courage and devotion to liberty.

In the beginning, before the white man came, Texas belonged to the Indians. A group of tribes of the Caddo nation northeast of San Antonio gave the vast territory its name, "Texas." The Caddo tribes called themselves *tejas,* or "friends." And *tejas* be-

Colonel William Barret Travis

came "Texas" among the early Spanish explorers of the region.

The great Texas land mass of some 268,000 square miles was claimed by Spain between 1519 and 1542. The Spaniards were the first white people the Indians of the region had ever seen. The Spaniards arrived with the first horses the Indians had ever seen, too. During this twenty-three-year period, the Spanish did a considerable amount of exploring. The Texas shoreline was mapped by Captain Alonso Álvarez de Piñeda, who sailed to the Gulf Coast from a Spanish base on the Caribbean island of Jamaica. Also, a handful of shipwrecked Spaniards led by Álvar Núñez Cabeza de Vaca (c. 1490–1557) walked over much of southern Texas. And Francisco Vásquez de Coronado (1510–1554) and Hernando de Soto (c. 1500–1542) took expeditions from Mexico into Texas looking for gold. They found none. Other than establishing a couple of Franciscan missions in the far western corner of Texas in 1682, the Spaniards were almost content to leave Texas to its native Indians. Those first mission huts were built by the friars to convert the Indians to Christianity. Were it not for French explorations in the area, the Spaniards might not have become so intent on bringing their civilization to Texas as quickly as they did.

In 1685, a Frenchman named Robert Cavalier, Sieur de La Salle (1643–1687), began to look for gold and silver inland from Matagorda Bay in southeastern Texas. As the French expeditions continued, the Spaniards began to build a string of missions and *presidios* (forts) to strengthen their hold on Texas. The French claimed Texas as their own. But La Salle died and the French withdrew. A year later, an expedition led by Domingo de Teran-Damian Manazanet, the first governor of Spanish Texas, camped on the banks of a river in the present-day San Antonio area.

"I named it San Antonio de Padua," he noted in his diary on June 13, 1691, "because we reached it on his day."

Spanish exploration

Fathers Antonio Olivares and Isidro Espinosa

Now the river had a Spanish name. But eighteen years later, two Spanish priests, Antonio Olivares and Isidro Espinosa, camped on the same riverbank.

"This river has not been named by the Spaniards," Father Espinosa wrote, "so we called it Rio de San Antonio de Padua."

A surprising event, this second naming of the San Antonio River. No one seemed to remember that it had been named before—and with the same name, no less.

Father Olivares liked the site. He asked for a transfer from his mission on the Rio Grande River, San Francisco Solano, which he thought was too dry, to this new place on the San Antonio River. His request was granted. On May 1, 1718, a stick-and-straw hut was built on the west bank of the San Antonio River. This was the new mission, San Antonio de Valero, named for the viceroy of Mexico, the Marquis de Valero. A few days later, on May 5, a town and a fort were founded nearby—Villa de Bejar and Presidio de Bejar. The town and the fort were named for the Marquis de Valero's brother, the Duke of Bejar.

Neither the mission nor the fort remained very long where they were first founded. Spain and the Catholic Church had developed a policy regarding the site and construction of the Spanish missions in the Americas as well as the location of the *presidios*. The Church and the government agreed that they would both be responsible for the mission. The government and the Church would share in the building of a walled enclosure to contain a chapel and convent or living quarters. All of this could be fortified and used as a military defense position if necessary. The Spanish government agreed also to protect the missions. In that regard, it was decided that the missions should not be located more than "2 cannon shots"—about a half mile—away from the *presidio*.

By 1727, the Mission of San Antonio de Valero, no longer a stick-and-straw hut, was bringing religion and civilization to about three hundred local Indians. Within fifty years, Bejar, although only a village, had become the capital of Spanish Texas. The mission continued to re-educate the Indian population according to Spanish and European ideas for the next sixty-six years. There were several other missions built along the San Antonio River as well. And each of these was established to do the same thing: maintain Spanish power in the area, convert the local Indians to Christianity, and teach them the crafts of European civilization like spinning, sewing, farming, and carpentry.

The plan of the mission was well defined by Spanish authorities. It consisted of a large plaza or yard surrounded by a wall, a stone chapel, a stone convent with its own backyard for the friars, and a row of rooms built into the walls to house the Indians whom the friars were trying to convert. Also, and as in most Spanish missions, there were places within the compound for various essential crafts like blacksmithing and tanning. A ditch

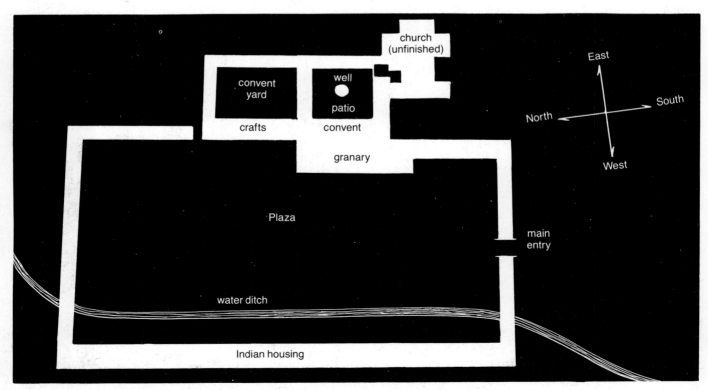

Plan of the Mission of San Antonio de Valero, circa 1750

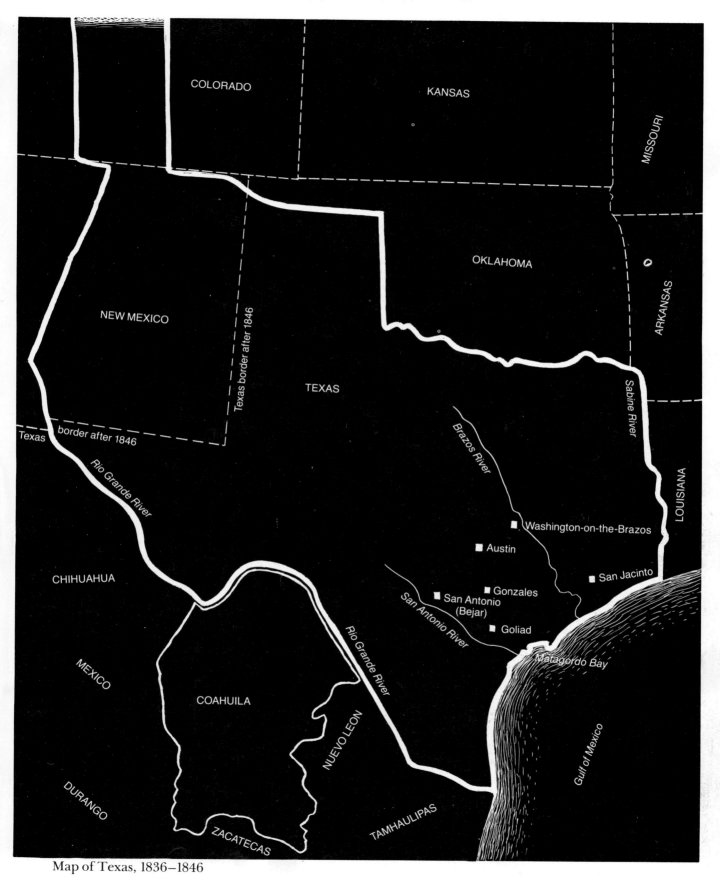

Map of Texas, 1836–1846

15

brought water from the San Antonio River into the compound.

By 1793, however, the Franciscan fathers who ran the Mission of San Antonio de Valero had moved away. Most of the local Indians had drifted off as well, uninterested in the efforts of the Franciscan fathers to convert them to Christianity. The friars allowed the mission's walled property to be used by the few Indians who remained there, including the unfinished stone chapel begun behind the mission walls thirty-five years before. At the time the friars left the mission, there were no more than six to seven thousand white settlers in all of Texas. By 1800, the mission was deserted even by the Indians. Only the alamos—the cottonwood trees—that grew around the mission seemed to bear witness to its history.

Not all was so peaceful farther south in Mexico. Discontent was everywhere among the Indians. Armed rebellion broke out in Mexico itself. Between 1810 and 1817, the Mexican Indians revolted without success against their Spanish masters, who had been ruling Mexico for almost three hundred years. An army of one hundred thousand Indians led by Father Miguel Hidalgo y Costillo, a half-Spanish, half-Indian Catholic priest, formed the heart of the rebellion. Nine years before that bloody time, the Spanish had transferred a regular army cavalry company from El Alamo, Mexico, to Bejar—the Second Volunteer Company of San Carlos de Parras—to protect the region from wild and hostile local Indians, if there was to be one, from spreading to that region. The horse soldiers occupied the Mission of San Antonio de Valero for the next twenty-four years, 1801 to 1825. They used it as a headquarters and barracks. Now, no longer a mission run by the Church, it was given a new name by the Spanish government. It was called "Pueblo del Alamo" (Alamo Village)—the Alamo, for short—after the Mexican town that had been the previous home of the cavalry unit.

Drawing of the Alamo in 1829 by José Juan Sanchez Estrada,
Engineer Officer, Mexican Army

Mexico declared a free and independent country

But no matter how quiet it seemed in Bejar and the Spanish province of Texas, resistance to Spanish rule in Mexico roared on for three more years. Determined to crush the rebels once and for all, the Spaniards sent an expedition in December 1820 against the last armed holdouts. The expedition was commanded by a Mexican-born Spanish army officer, Augustin de Iturbide (1783–1824). Instead of crushing this last pocket of rebellion, Iturbide joined the rebels as their leader. Nine months later, in September 1821, Iturbide and his men ended Spanish rule in Mexico. Mexico was declared a free and independent country. Spain's former provinces, Texas included, were now Mexican provinces. Iturbide, the new strongman, had himself proclaimed Emperor Augustin I of Mexico in 1822.

The Mexican turmoil, however, did not end with Spanish defeat. The Mexican people did not want an emperor with absolute power over them. They had just kicked Spain out of Mexico for that very same reason. Iturbide was no different from the cruel Spanish viceroys who had ruled before. He faced an outraged people in 1823 and lost his imperial position. A year later, Mexico adopted a constitution and became a republic. Guadalupe Victoria (circa 1786–1843) was elected Mexico's first president.

Still, the country boiled over with plots and counterplots and again with revolution. Mexican army officers schemed against the president and each other to seize power. None of them were interested in improving the lot of the people; they only wanted to improve their own lot. In their personal ambition and lust for power, none of these military conspirators paid the least attention to Mexico's northernmost province—Texas. There, colonists, or *empresarios,* from the United States were beginning to live on land granted by the Mexicans. A few small Texas towns were being filled out by these American *empresarios* from over the border.

By 1830 there were some thirty thousand American settlers in

Mexico's Texas. And they brought with them a thirst for adventure and the frontier, a spirit of independence, elective government, and personal liberty, generated by the American Declaration of Independence and the United States Constitution.

The burgeoning American emigration into Texas worried the Mexicans about American intentions. So, in 1830, the Mexicans prohibited any further land grants to Americans. The ban infuriated Americans who had already settled there. The Mexicans had good cause to worry about the growing American movement westward into Texas. France had claimed the Texas territory ever since the La Salle expeditions into southeastern Texas during the late 1600s. But France never did anything to assert its sovereignty over Texas. So far as Spain—and, later, Mexico—was concerned, Texas was in no way a French territory settled permanently by French people under the flag of the French king. Nor had it ever been. Yet, when the French emperor, Napoleon Bonaparte, sold the Louisiana Territory to the young United States in 1803 to finance his European wars, the United States said that Texas was also French. And since Spain did not have sole claim over Texas to begin with, according to some American politicians, the United States preferred to recognize the French claim of the 1680s to suit its own territorial aims. The whole thing was far-fetched. But the United States made its point. It had its eye on Texas.

Like France, the United States did little to assert its sovereignty over Texas. Instead, adventurous Americans settled in the Mexican province, not knowing that one day there would be enough American presence and pressure to make Texas an American territory—perhaps even a state.

Chief among the young army officers trying to grab Mexico for themselves was Antonio López de Santa Anna. He was the same Santa Anna who would soon force the American settlers to act at

state boundary lines are modern

dashed line: territory ceded to Spain in 1819

Map of the Louisiana Purchase, 1803

the Alamo, and who would lose Texas as a Mexican province. Santa Anna connived to have himself made president of Mexico in 1833. Over the next twenty-two years, Santa Anna would fall in and out of the presidency four times, becoming, in the process, an absolute ruler, the dictator of Mexico.

It was Santa Anna's seizure of all government powers in 1835 that triggered the chain of events that would enshrine the old mission—the Alamo—in American hearts forever. Santa Anna had discarded the Mexican constitution and replaced it with his own rule of law. He called himself the "Napoleon of the West." American colonists from the east who had sworn allegiance to Mexico now felt betrayed. Two years earlier, Santa Anna had angered Texan Americans when he imprisoned Stephen F. Austin (1793–1836), the leading colonist. Austin had sought out Santa Anna in Mexico City over Texas territorial status. The Mexicans had combined Texas with the Mexican state of Coahuila, causing Texans to lose their voice in Mexican affairs under Santa Anna's rule. After presenting the president with a petition to restore Texas to Mexican statehood, Austin was thrown in prison for treason without a trial. There he remained for a year and a half. With Austin's jailing fresh in their minds, the once angered Texans—Americans, Mexicans, and Spaniards—were now enraged. The Indian population—mostly hostile Comanches and Apaches—had little to say in the developing trouble. The Comanches, in particular, had been raiding non-Indian settlements in a century-old effort to drive the white people from the land the Indians claimed as their own.

"War is our only resource," Austin wrote to his fellow Texans on September 19, 1835. "There is no other remedy but to defend our rights, our country, and ourselves by force of arms."

By 1835, there were five thousand Hispanics—Mexican or Spanish—in Texas. There were also thirty-five thousand white and black Americans. The population of the United States at the

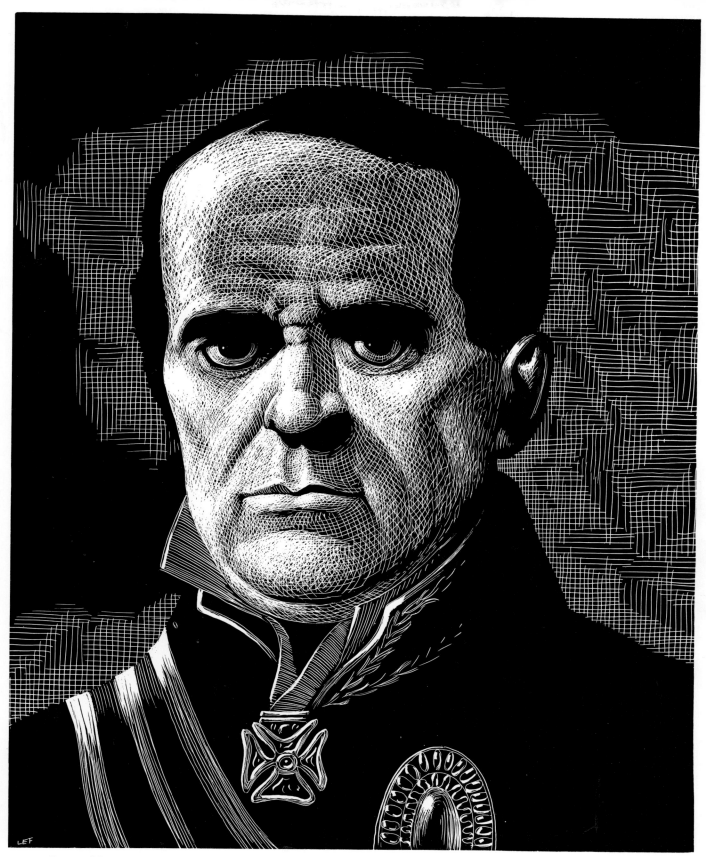

General Santa Anna

time numbered about thirteen million. One out of every four hundred thirty-three Americans was in Texas!

Austin's call to arms brought the entire Texan-American community and most of the Texan-Hispanic community together in revolt against Mexico and Santa Anna. Some of this revolutionary activity to separate Texas from Mexico was around Bejar—soon to be called San Antonio—formerly in Texas but now in the state of Coahuila. But the hub of the rebellion was in Washington-on-the-Brazos, a town one hundred fifty miles northeast of Bejar.

The ink on Austin's letter was hardly dry when an alarmed Santa Anna sent his brother-in-law, General Martín Perfecto de Cos, with twelve hundred Mexican troops and twenty-one cannons to occupy Bejar. The general came with orders to arrest anyone opposed to Santa Anna, to disarm the Texans, and to send all Americans who had been in Bejar less than five years back to the United States.

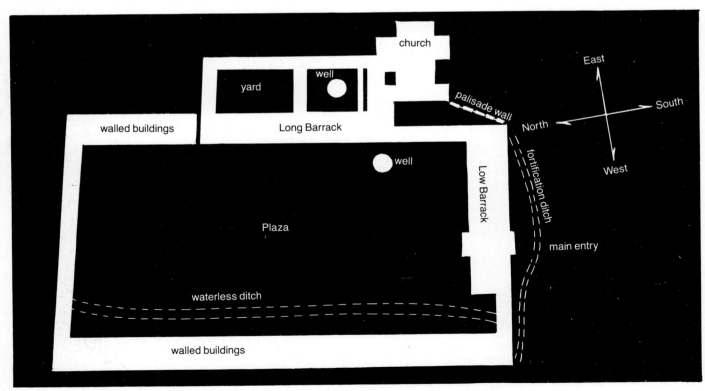

Plan of the Alamo, 1835–1836

Stephen Fuller Austin

De Cos put six hundred troops in the vacant Alamo and six hundred at a barricade in the main plaza—the center—of Bejar. The Mexicans removed the roof of the Alamo chapel and piled the pieces under a mound of dirt against the east or back wall. This enabled them to haul three cannons up the ramplike mound to the top of the chapel's rear wall.

Meanwhile, on October 2, at Gonzales, a tiny town about sixty-five miles east of Bejar, a Mexican cavalry officer, Lieutenant Francisco Castañeda, and one hundred troopers, demanded that a band of one hundred sixty Texans surrender their only cannon. "Come and take it," the Texans cried, and fired a single shot. The Mexicans fled. The war was on. Volunteers for the fight streamed into Gonzales. A number under the command of Stephen F. Austin went to the outskirts of Bejar to join the volunteers gathering there. Here, too, were the one hundred members of the New Orleans Greys, a United States volunteer force. They had marched from New Orleans to reinforce the meager Texas army

Cannon shot at Gonzales, October 2, 1835

Flag of the New Orleans Greys, 1835

now being formed to attack de Cos.

While de Cos waited and four hundred armed Texans gathered outside of Bejar, fifty-seven other Texans had written and signed a Declaration of Causes explaining why they were now going to war against Mexico for their independence. The word came on November 7, 1835:

> Whereas, General Antonio López de Santa Anna, and other military chieftains, have by force of arms overthrown the federal institutions of Mexico, and dissolved the social compact which existed between Texas and other members of the Mexican confederacy; now the good people of Texas, availing themselves of their natural rights, Solemnly Declare:
>
> That they have taken up arms in defense of their rights and liberties, which were threatened by the encroachments of military despots, and in defense of the republican principles of the federal constitution of Mexico, 1824.
>
> That Texas is no longer morally or civilly bound by the compact of union; yet, stimulated by the generosity and sympathy common to a free people, they offer their support and assistance to such members of the Mexican confederacy as will take up arms against military despotism.
>
> That they hold it to be their right during the disorganization of the federal system, and the reign of despotism, to withdraw from the union, and to establish an independent government . . .

Among the signers of the Declaration of Causes was Sam Houston (1793–1863), who, less than a year later, would be elected the first president of the Republic of Texas.

At daybreak, December 5, three hundred men of the Army of Texas attacked de Cos at the main plaza barricade in Bejar and at the Alamo. A few days later, on December 8, de Cos hoisted a white flag over the Alamo. The Battle of Bejar was over. De Cos

Declaration of Causes, November 7, 1835
ARCHIVES DIVISION, TEXAS STATE LIBRARY

DECLARACION
DEL PUEBLO DE TEJAS,
Reunido en Convencion General.

POR CUANTO el general Antonio Lopez de Santa Ana, asociado con otros gefes militares han destruido por medio de la fuerza armada las Instituciones Federales de la Nacion Mejicana, y disuelto el pacto social que existia entre el Pueblo de Tejas y las demas partes de la confederacion Mejicana, el buen Pueblo de Tejas, usando de sus derechos naturales,

DECLARA SOLEMNEMENTE,

Primero. Que ha tomado las armas en defensa de sus derechos y libertades amenezados por los ataques del despotismo militar; y en defensa de lós principios republicanos de la Constitucion Federal de Mejico, sancionada en 1824.

Segundo. Que aunque Tejas no está ya ni politica ni moralmente ligado por los lazos de la Union Federal, movido por la simpatia y generosidad naturales á los pueblos libres, ofrece ayuda y asistencia á aquellos miembros de la confederacion que tomasen las armas contra el despotismo militar.

Tercero. Que no reconoce en las actuales autoridades de la *nominal* Republica Mejicana ningun derecho para gobernar en el territorio de Tejas.

Cuarto. Que no cesará de hacer la guerra contra las mencionadas autoridades mientras mantengan tropas en los terminos de Tejas.

Quinto. Que se considera con derecho de separarse de la Union á Mejico durante la desorganizacion del Sistema Federal y el regimen del despotismo, y para organizar un gobierno independiente ó adoptar aquellas medidas que sean adecuadas para proteger sus derechos y libertades; pero continuará fiel al gobierno Mejicano en el caso de que la nacion sea gobernada por la Constitucion y las leyes que fueron formadas para el regimen de su asociacion politica.

Sesto. Que Tejas se obliga á pagar los gastos de sus tropas en actividad actualmente en la campaña.

Septimo. Que Tejas empeña su credito y fé publica para el pago de las deudas que contrageren sus agentes.

Octavo. Que recompensará con donaciones de tierra y los derechos de ciudadania á los voluntarios que prestasen servicios en la presente lucha.

Esta es la declaracion que profesamos delante del mundo, llamando á Dios por testigo de la sinceridad de nuestras intenciones, invocando su maldicion sobre nuestras cabezas en el caso de faltar á ella por doblez ó intencion dañada.

B. T. ARCHER, *Presidente.*

Municipalidad de Austin.
THOMAS BARNETT,
WYLY MARTIN,
RANDALL JONES,
WM. MENIFEE,
JESSE BURNAM.

Municipalidad de Matagorda.
R. R. ROYALL,
CHARLES WILSON.

Municipalidad de Washington.
ASA MITCHELL,
PHILIP COE,
ELIJAH COLLARD,
JESSE GRIMES,
A. HOXIE.

Municipalidad de Mina.
J. S. LESTER,
D. C. BARRETT,
R. M. WILLIAMSON.

Municipalidad de Columbia.
HENRY SMITH,
EDWIN WALLER,
J. S. D. BYROM,
JOHN A. WHARTON,
W. D. C. HALL.

Municipalidad de Harrisburgh.
LORENZO DE ZAVALA,
WM. P. HARRIS,
C. C. DYER,
MERIWETHER W. SMITH,
JOHN W. MOORE,
D. B. MACOMB.

Municipalidad de Gonzales.
J. D. CLEMENS,
BENJAMIN FUQUA,
JAMES HODGES,
WILLIAM ARRINGTON,
WILLIAM S. FISHER,
G. W. DAVIS.

Municipalidad de Viesca.
S. T. ALLEN,
A. G. PERRY,
J. G. W. PIERSON,
ALEXANDER THOMPSON,
J. W. PARKER.

Municipalidad de Nacogdoches.
SAMUEL HOUSTON,
DANIEL PARKER,
JAMES W. ROBERTSON,
WILLIAM WHITAKER.

Municipality of Bevil.
JOHN BEVIL,
S. H. EVERETT,
WYATT HANKS.

Municipalidad de San Augustin.
A. HOUSTON,
WM. N. SIGLER,
A. E. C. JOHNSON,
A. HORTON,
MARTIN PALMER,
HENRY AUGUSTIN,
A. G. KELLOGG.

Municipalidad de Liberty.
J. B. WOODS,
A. B. HARDIN,
HENRY MILLARD,
C. WEST.

P. B. DEXTER, *Secretario.*

Sala de la Convencion en San Felipe de Austin, 7 de Noviembre de 1825.

En la imprenta de Baker y Bordens, San Felipe de Austin.

Sam Houston

surrendered all Mexican property, arms, and ammunition, agreeing to move his troops south of the Rio Grande and never to fight Texans again. It was a promise he did not keep.

For their part, the victorious Texans took over the Alamo, now a fortress, and began maintaining a garrison there. What used to be the mission convent became a barracks and was called the Long Barrack. The upper floor, or what was left of it after the Battle of Bejar, became the garrison hospital.

Santa Anna, enraged and alarmed over the defeat of his brother-in-law, General de Cos, personally took command of a four thousand-man army and headed north to Bejar. He would have his revenge. Seated in a saddle trimmed with glittering gold, a great sword dangling at his side, Santa Anna arrived at the main plaza on the afternoon of February 23. The bells of the Church of San Fernando signaled his presence after a month's journey from Mexico City. He ordered a red flag to be hoisted

Arrival of Santa Anna

from the belfry of San Fernando Church. It was the demand to surrender or be killed.

The defenders of Bejar—one hundred eighty-eight men under the joint command of Colonel Travis and Colonel James Bowie (1795–1836), a Bejar resident—had barricaded themselves in the Alamo. Upon sighting the red flag, Travis fired a cannon shot at the Mexicans. There would be no surrender.

Also waiting inside the Alamo with a company of Tennessee volunteers was the famous frontiersman, backwoods rifleman, and three-term congressman from Tennessee, David Crockett (1786–1836). Two weeks earlier, Crockett, standing on a box in Bejar's main plaza, told a worried audience badly in need of encouragement, "I have come to aid you all that I can in your noble cause . . . and all the honor I desire is that of defending . . . the liberties of our common country."

Davy Crockett talks to a crowd in Bejar

Davy Crockett, painted by John Gadsey Chapman, 1834

Bowie, another well-known frontiersman and Indian fighter, commanded the "Bejar Volunteers" in the Alamo. They were reinforced by thirty soldiers under the command of Colonel Travis and Davy Crockett's fourteen men. The twenty-seven-year-old Travis, a lawyer and a lieutenant colonel in the Army of Texas, was considered the senior officer. But Bowie's volunteers refused to serve under him. They thought Travis was too young. A compromise was reached by establishing a joint command. But Bowie became deathly sick and lay in his quarters in the Low Barrack. He had pneumonia and had to be carried everywhere on a litter. The day after Santa Anna's arrival, Jim Bowie gave up his command to the young Travis. Crockett was made a colonel of the Alamo garrison but it was chiefly an honorary rank. A week later, thirty-two volunteers from Gonzales, responding to Colonel Travis's letter of February 24, 1836, pleading for help, sneaked into the Alamo.

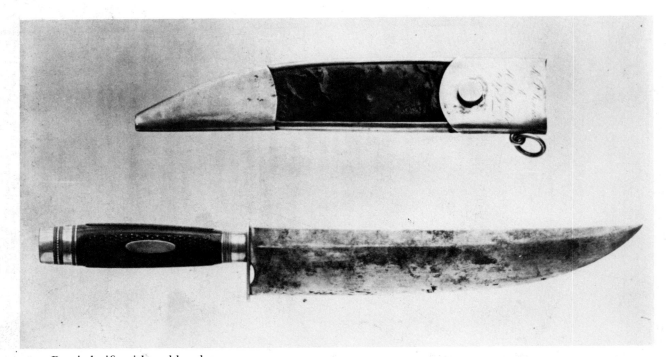

Bowie knife with scabbard

Colonel James Bowie U.T. INSTITUTE OF
TEXAN CULTURES AT SAN ANTONIO

By this time the Mexicans were keeping up a steady bombardment of the Alamo. They were moving in closer and taking a measure of the Alamo's defenses for a final assault. Alamo cannons returned the Mexican fire, ripping at the Mexican lines and encampment. From time to time the Mexicans were astonished to hear the shrill and mournful tones of a bagpipe or the scratchy notes of a fiddle float above the settling cannon smoke. The musical interludes were unexpected responses to the sounds of thudding cannon fire and crackling rifles. The fiddler was Davy Crockett. The piper was John McGregor, a Scotsman who had settled in Texas and joined its fight for freedom.

The people of Texas answered Santa Anna's guns, too. While Travis's men were barricaded in the Alamo, they declared Texas a free and independent nation. On March 2, 1836, delegates from fifty-nine Texas towns signed a Declaration of Independence. In it they complained of Mexican government oppression, unjustified imprisonment of Texans, no trial by jury, no public educa-

Cabin in Washington-on-the-Brazos, Texas, where Declaration of Independence was signed

The fiddler and the piper

Alamo.

Villita.

Bejar.

Campo Santo.

38

Santa Anna's map of the Alamo, prepared by
Colonel Ygnacio de Labistida, Mexican Army
Engineers, March 1836

Susanna Dickinson, survivor of the Alamo massacre,
wife of Almeron Dickinson from Tennessee,
who died at the Alamo

tion, and no freedom of religion. Most Texans were Protestants, but Catholicism was the official religion of Mexico. The Mexican government made life difficult for non-Catholics.

Catholic or not the one hundred eighty-eight bone-weary defenders of the Alamo could not hold back the Mexican tide that came over and through the stone walls in the morning darkness of March 6, 1836. But they hung on stubbornly—from the plaza to the Long Barrack, in one room and out the other—fighting hand to hand with pistols, rifle butts, knives, bayonets, sticks, and fists, until they had all died.

Francisco Antonio Ruiz, the mayor of Bejar—now called San Antonio—described what he saw:

"On the north battery of the fortress lay the lifeless body of Colonel Travis on the gun carriage, shot only in the forehead. Toward the west, and in the small fort opposite the city, we found the body of Colonel Crockett. Colonel Bowie was found dead in

TEXAS!!

Emigrants who are desirious of assisting Texas at this important crisis of her affairs may have a free passage and equipments, by applying at the

NEW-YORK and PHILADELPHIA HOTEL,

On the Old Levee, near the Blue Stores.

Now is the time to ensure a fortune in Land: To all who remain in Texas during the War will be allowed 1280 Acres.
To all who remain Six Months, 640 Acres.
To all who remain Three Months, 320 Acres.
And as Colonists, 4600 Acres for a family and 1470 Acres for a Single Man.
New Orleans, April 23d, 1836.

Battle of the Alamo

his bed, in one of the rooms of the south side. . . ."

When told of her son's death, Mrs. Rezin Bowie remarked, "I'll wager they found no wounds in his back."

The fighting between Mexico and Texas went on. But not at the Alamo. Santa Anna took his victorious army to Goliad, a town about ninety miles southeast of San Antonio. Again he bloodied the Texans. Three hundred and ninety-three Texans survived the battle and surrendered on March 19, 1836. Among the prisoners were about sixty wounded. Eight days later all three hundred ninety three were executed by Santa Anna's troops.

Confident of final victory, Santa Anna continued to pursue the rebellious Texans eastward to San Jacinto, on the site of present-day Houston, Texas. The terrified general population fled before him. But there, on April 21, 1836, General Sam Houston and seven hundred eighty-three Texans surprised the fifteen hundred-man advanced group of Santa Anna's army. Having first cut off any escape route by blowing up a bridge, thus preventing the main Mexican army from reinforcing them, Sam Houston and his men fell upon the Mexicans with unrelieved fury.

"Remember the Alamo!" "Remember Goliad!" screamed the charging, enraged Texans.

Eighteen minutes later, six hundred thirty Mexicans were dead and the rest were taken prisoner—among them Santa Anna. Only nine Texans died in the short battle. The war for Texas independence was over. The Republic of Texas was truly a free country. It no longer belonged to Mexico. All that remained was for both governments—Mexico and Texas—to work out the arrangements and terms of Texas sovereignty. There were treaties and agreements. The United States immediately recognized Texas, as did England, France, and other European nations. But it took the Mexicans until 1848, another twelve years, to finally give Texas the same recognition. During that time, on February 19, 1846,

Texas gave up its independence and became part of the United States, entering the Union as the twenty-eighth state.

Santa Anna continued to be a nuisance not only to Texas and, later, to Texan Americans, but to his own Mexican countrymen as well. After signing a treaty giving Texas to Texans, General Santa Anna was set free by Sam Houston. When he returned to Mexico City, he was turned out of office as president for having lost Texas. However, he returned several more times as president. When Mexico and the United States went to war in 1846 over a continuing territorial dispute, Santa Anna commanded the Mexican army. He was defeated by the Americans three times—at Buena Vista, Cerro Gordo, and Chapultepec. Finally, Mexico City itself fell and Santa Anna fled the country. He returned a few years later to become president again, only to be kicked out of office and out of the country. It would be a long time before Mexico would allow him to come home. In 1874, nearly eighty

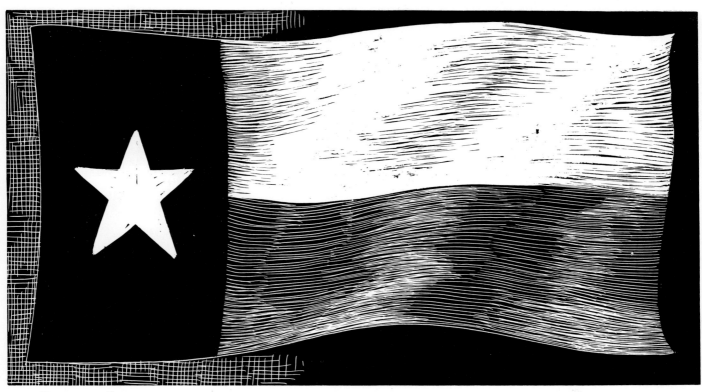

Texas state flag

Alamo ruins drawn by Edward Everett, 1846

years old, Santa Anna did return to Mexico City, where he died a poor and broken man.

The fate of the Alamo, where so few sacrificed so much, was uncertain. Shortly after the thirteen-day siege in 1836, it seemed as if the Alamo would linger only as a rubble of stone. No one paid much attention to the site as the national shrine it has become today. Still, most everyone knew that an important battle had been fought there, and that the Texans who fought and died there would be heroes until the end of time.

The Alamo now belonged to the young Texas Republic. The Catholic Church, which had allowed a few local Indians to use the property some forty years before, wanted the Alamo returned so that it could become a house of worship. In 1842, Texas returned the Alamo to the Church. Unfortunately, the Church was unable to restore the Alamo as a religious place of worship.

In 1847, eleven years following the massacre, the Church rented the Alamo to the United States government. United States army forces in the area needed it as a supply depot. And with the Church's blessing and permission, American soldiers began to restore the Alamo for military use. By 1849, the Alamo chapel had a new roof. In addition, the Americans added a rounded architectural element with two new side windows above the main entrance of the chapel. This new look to the building's facade gave it the appearance familiar to present-day visitors. Also, the army refurbished the Long Barrack for a variety of purposes. Here they stored weapons and medical supplies. They also maintained command offices, a saddler's shop, and a stable.

When the Civil War (1861–1864) broke out, Confederate forces occupied San Antonio. The federal troops still assigned to the Alamo were forced to surrender the post. The newly vacated Alamo was assigned to the Alamo City Guards under the command of Captain William M. Edgar. The Alamo City Guard was

The earliest known photograph of the Alamo, 1850

The Alamo, circa 1868, U.T. INSTITUTE OF TEXAN CULTURES AT SAN ANTONIO

a local San Antonio military group charged with the Alamo's defense against any federal attack, which never happened. Between 1861 and 1864, the Alamo was a quiet Confederate garrison.

When the war ended and southern General Robert E. Lee (1807–1870) surrendered at the Appomatox Courthouse in Virginia to northern General Ulysses S. Grant (1822–1885), the Alamo was returned to the United States Army. The army renewed its lease with the Catholic Church, which still owned the property, and once again used the Alamo as a supply depot.

The United States Army remained at the Alamo for the next twelve years, until 1876, when a new supply depot was built at Fort Sam Houston in San Antonio. The fort was named in honor of the first president of the Texas Republic, the state's first governor, and the general who whipped Santa Anna. It was established as a small army post in San Antonio in 1850, three years after the United States government had rented the Alamo as a supply depot.

With the army gone from the Alamo, the Catholic Church looked around for either a new tenant or a new owner. The Church found one in the person of Honoré Grenet, a merchant. Grenet turned out to be both tenant and owner. He bought the Long Barrack and its courtyard outright in 1877. Over this large area he built a huge wood-frame general store with several castle-like towers. Meant to be imposing, the entire structure was soon dubbed Grenet's "Palace." But Grenet needed a warehouse to store his supplies and salable items. The Church obliged by allowing him to rent the Alamo chapel. Between 1877 and 1883, and beyond the great expanse of the Alamo plaza, stood the familiar chapel with Grenet's Palace on the chapel's right; and the Alamo Beer Garden, Saloon, Restaurant on the chapel's left. The City Meat Market stood in the center of the Alamo Plaza. The people of San Antonio and the rest of Texas were beginning to

Alamo Beer Garden, Saloon, Restaurant, circa 1880

Alamo plaza with the city meat market, circa 1883

Alamo plaza, circa 1885

have second thoughts about the undignified fate of the Alamo, the focus of Texas history.

A campaign to save the Alamo from commercial blight and restore it to a respectful place among the heroic shrines of America slowly began to emerge. In 1883, the State of Texas purchased the Alamo chapel for $20,000 from the Catholic Church. Grenet lost his warehouse. Two years later, in 1885, Texas turned the chapel over to the City of San Antonio.

Meanwhile, Honoré Grenet had died. And in the same year that the City of San Antonio had become custodian of the Alamo chapel—1885—Grenet's Palace and all of the property it contained, including the Long Barrack, was sold to a department store company, Hugo & Schmeltzer. The company continued to run the store for nineteen years. In 1903, it began to look for a buyer who might want to turn the property into a hotel.

The idea of a hotel built on such historic ground moved the Daughters of the Republic of Texas to save the site as a historic monument. The Daughters of the Republic of Texas had been formed a few years earlier in 1891. The group's purpose was to preserve the history of the fight for Texas independence, the memory of those who won it, and the historic places—such as the Alamo—that are sacred to the struggle for Texas freedom. The members of the organization are all direct descendants of those who fought in the Texas Revolution. In 1904, a chapter of the Daughters, led by Adina de Zavala, whose grandfather was a vice-president of the Republic of Texas, began a fund-raising project to raise the $75,000 needed to buy the Hugo & Schmeltzer property and keep it from becoming a hotel.

The chapter could not raise enough money. The project to preserve and restore the Alamo looked hopeless until wealthy twenty-three-year-old Clara Driscoll (1881–1945), whose grandfathers fought at the Battle of San Jacinto, bought the property

Adina de Zavala

Alamo plaza on July 4, 1898

Clara Driscoll

herself. A year later, in 1905, Clara Driscoll gave her purchase to the State of Texas. The state returned to her the same amount of money she had spent on the purchase and appointed the Daughters of the Republic of Texas guardians of the Alamo. The historic property was entrusted entirely to their care. And by agreement, they would provide the necessary money to maintain the Alamo, the shrine of Texas liberty, rather than seek such funds from the State of Texas. And this they have done, without charging fees of admission.

The property that comprises the Alamo today—a little over four acres—was named a national historic landmark by the United States government in 1960. The Alamo continues to grow in the minds of Americans, not so much as the site of a heroic defense of freedom as for the heroic courage it took to stand up and die for that freedom.

Seal of the Daughters of the Republic of Texas

Present-day aerial view of the Alamo and environs

THE ALAMO.
SAN ANTONIO. TEXAS.

Facade of the Alamo chapel (Mission San Antonio de Valero) after 1850

Index

(Italicized numbers indicate pages with photos.)

Alamo ruins drawn by J. Edmund Blake, 1845

ACKNOWLEDGMENTS

Leonard Everett Fisher wishes to thank the Daughters of the Republic of Texas; Edith Mae Johnson, Chairman of the Alamo Committee of the Daughters of the Republic of Texas; Steve W. Beck, Curator of the Alamo; Ed Gearke, Assistant to the Curator of the Alamo; and Bernice Strong, Librarian-Archivist of the Daughters of the Republic of Texas Library at the Alamo. Their assistance in the preparation and research for this book was invaluable; their patience was most appreciated. Without their guidance, Mr. Fisher could not have wandered through the Alamo and felt the spirit and surge of those who achieved so much for so many on that spot.

Mr. Fisher would also like to thank the Daughters of the Republic of Texas Library for supplying, and granting permission to reprint, the photos on pages 1, 2, 4–5, 6, 9, 17, 27, 29, 30, 33, 34, 35, 38–39, 40, 41, 46–47, 49 (top and bottom), 51 (top and bottom), 52–53, 55, 56–57, 58, 60–61, 62, and 64.

Mr. Fisher drew the scratchboard drawings which appear on pages 11, 12, 14, 15, 18, 21, 23, 24, 25, 26, 31, 32, 36, 37, 42–43, 45, and 59.

Library of Congress Cataloging-in-Publication Data

Fisher, Leonard Everett.
The Alamo.

Includes index.
SUMMARY: A history of the building well known as a fortress during Texas's fight for independence, which has also served as a mission, barracks, military supply post, warehouse, and general store.
1. Alamo (San Antonio, Tex.)—Juvenile literature. 2. Texas—History—To 1846—Juvenile literature. 3. San Antonio (Tex.)—Buildings, structures, etc.—Juvenile literature. [1. Alamo (San Antonio, Tex.) 2. Texas—History—To 1846. 3. San Antonio (Tex.)—Buildings, structures, etc.] I. Title.
F390.F532   1987   976.4′351   86-46204
ISBN 0-8234-0646-6

64